Rosemary Cass-Beggs read philosophy and psychology at Somerville College, Oxford. She has worked in the field of social research at the Tavistock Institute of Human Relations, London, and at the Canadian Centre for Community Studies and the Royal Commission on the Status of Women in Canada, Ottawa. She now tutors for the Open University and lectures for the Department of Adult Education at the University of Surrey. She is the child of one professional musician and the sister of another; her interest in rounds dates from her childhood. She is married to Dr M. Burstall and lives in Guildford.

THE PENGUIN
BOOK OF
ROUNDS

Rosemary Cass-Beggs

Penguin Books

Penguin Books Ltd, Harmondsworth, Middlesex, England
Penguin Books, 625 Madison Avenue, New York, New York, U.S.A.
Penguin Books Australia Ltd, Ringwood, Victoria, Australia
Penguin Books Canada Ltd, 2801 John Street, Markham, Ontario, Canada L3R 1B4
Penguin Books (N.Z.) Ltd, 182-190 Wairau Road, Auckland 10, New Zealand

First published 1982
Copyright © Rosemary Cass-Beggs, 1982
Music artwork by Roger Brison and Clifford Caesar

Made and printed in Great Britain by
Hazell Watson & Viney Ltd, Aylesbury, Bucks
Set in Times New Roman

TO MY PARENTS

Contents

Introduction

According to Thomas Ravenscroft, writing in 1609, rounds provide 'harmony to please, variety to delight, facility to invite thee'. Rounds are easy to sing, for all voices sing the same tune. This is their inviting *facility*. The *harmony* comes from the way the tune is constructed: it is made up of three or more short sections which will produce a pleasing sound if they are sung together. In singing a round, then, each voice starts to sing the tune a short time after another has begun, until all three (or four, or it might be ten) sections are being sung together. The effect is as satisfying as that of any part-song but achieved so much more simply. The only difficulty, in fact, lies in finding rounds to sing. Hundreds of rounds were published in England between the sixteenth and nineteenth centuries. They were sung in the clubs and taverns, where enthusiasts gathered much as folk-song enthusiasts do today. But how many rounds do most of us know? Half a dozen, perhaps? In our time, we lack the *variety* Ravenscroft speaks of. It is the aim of this collection to fill the gap, to introduce today's singers to the wealth of English rounds.

For this collection, all the rounds have been transcribed from their earliest published form into modern spelling and musical notation. A very few, certain, errors have been corrected, but possible errors remain. Since the original key was often arbitrary or pitched to suit men's voices, most of the rounds have been transposed into a key that is easier for mixed voices to sing. Rounds on a similar topic have been grouped together and, within each section, are presented in chronological order. The date of their first publication, given beside the composer's name, identifies the particular source among the collections listed in Appendix 2. An outline of the history and development of the round in England is given in Appendix 1. All periods have their better and their worse examples. For this collection I have tried to avoid rounds which are tedious or awkward to sing, and those which are very long.

In singing rounds, the usual procedure is for each voice to sing the round completely through three times for a three-part round, four times for a four-part round, and so on. Another method is to stop, together, as soon as the *first* voice has sung the round three times. This method suits those rounds, usually long ones, in which the last notes of each section are designed to make a closing chord. Many rounds can be sung either way, however, and in singing from this book, singers should feel free to decide which method they prefer. Finally, singers should remember that rounds can always be sung by fewer voices than called for and that instrumentalists can play one, several, or all the parts, as you wish.

I The Fortunes of Love

1 Anon. (1609a)

1. Joan, come kiss me now,
2. Once a-gain for my love gen - tle
3. Joan come kiss me now.

2 Anon. (1609a)

1. Well fare the night - in - gale,
2. Fair fall the thrush - cock too, But foul
3. fare the fil - thy bird that sing - eth 'Cuc-koo'.

Note: Here and elsewhere the call of 'cuckoo' is taken to mean 'cuckold'.

3 Anon. (1609a)

1. Fare - well mine own sweet - heart,
2. Fare - well whom I love best,
3. Since I must from my love de - part,
4. A - dieu my joy and rest.

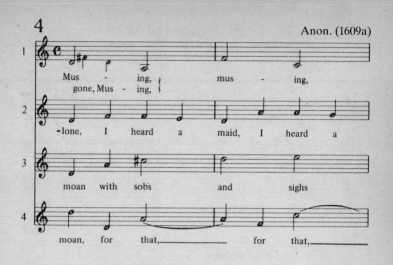

5

Anon. (1609a)

Hey ho, what shall I say, Sir John hath car - ried my wife a - way.
They were gone ere I wist, she will come when she list, hey trol - ly trol - ly lol - ly.
Come a - gain, ho.

6

Anon. (1609a)

1. As I me walk - èd
In a May morn - ing
I heard a bird sing:
Cuc - koo.

2. She nodded up and down
   And swore all by her crown
   She had friends in the town.
   Cuckoo.

3. All you that married be
   Learn this song of me
   So shall we not agree.
   Cuckoo.

4. All young men in this throng
   To marry that think it long
   Come learn of me this song.
   Cuckoo.

7

Anon. (1609a)

1. What hap had I to mar-ry a shrew,
For she hath given me ma-ny a blow,
And how to please her, a-lack I do not know.

2. From morn to e'en her tongue ne'er lies,
   Some time she brawls, some time she cries,
   Yet can I scarce keep her talons from my eyes.

3. If I go abroad and late come in,
   Sir knave, saith she, where have you been?
   And do I well or ill, she claps me on the skin.

8

1. Oa - ken leaves in the mer - ry wood so wild,
2. Fair - est maid, and thou be with child,
3. Lul - la lul - la-by lul-la lul-la lul-la-by,

when will you grow green, a,
lul - la - by mayest thou sing, a,
lul - la - by mayest thou sing, a.

9

Anon. (1609b)

1. O my love,
2. lov'st thou me? Then
3. quick - ly come and save him who
4. dies for thee.

Note: Ravenscroft gives this round in the major key. In Walsh's collection (1762), the round appears in the minor key. Take your pick.

10   Anon. (1762)

O my love,

lov'st thou me? Then

quick - ly come and save him who

dies for thee.

11   Anon. (1609b)

Go to Joan Glov - er and

tell her I love her and

at the mid of the moon

I will come to her.

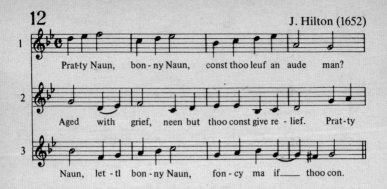

12   J. Hilton (1652)

1. Prat-ty Naun, bon-ny Naun, const thoo leuf an aude man?

2. Aged with grief, neen but thoo const give re - lief. Prat-ty

3. Naun, let-tl bon-ny Naun, fon-cy ma if___ thoo con.

Note: This was entitled 'A Northern Catch'. If you wish, ignore the dialect and sing in standard English. The tune is too beautiful to be missed.

13   W. Lawes (1652)

1. Ne-ver let a man take hea-vi-ly the

2. ruled by me and lead__ a mer - ry

3. thing, if she scolds then

cla - mour of his wife, but be

life. Let her have her will in ev' - ry

laugh___ and sing, hey der-ry der-ry der-ry ding.

14
J. Cranford (1652)

1. Here dwells a pret-ty maid whose name is

2. Her whole, her whole, her whole, her

3. ___ you may kiss, you may kiss, you may kiss,

Sis, you__ may come in and kiss.

whole es-tate is sev'n-teen pence a year. Yet__

you may kiss her if you come but near.

Note: This is an example of a particular form of catch where the words of one section interleave with those of another to provide a *double entendre*.

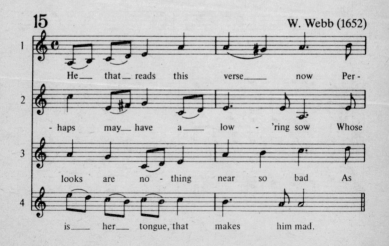

15
W. Webb (1652)

1. He__ that__ reads this verse___ now Per-

2. -haps may__ have a___ low - 'ring sow Whose

3. looks are no - thing near so bad As

4. is___ her__ tongue, that makes him mad.

16

J. Hilton (1652)

Turn, Am - a - ryl - lis, to thy swain, Thy

Here is a pret - ty, pret - ty, pret - ty ar - bour by, Where___

There let's sit and while I play,

Da - mon calls thee back a - gain.

___ A - pol - lo, where A - pol - lo can - not spy.

Sing to my pipes a - roun - de - lay.

17

Anon. (1652)

When - e - ver I mar - ry I'll mar - ry a maid,

I'll__ mar - ry a maid, for wi - dows are wil - ful,

for__ wi - dows are wil - ful and will be o - beyed.

18

J. Hilton (1652)

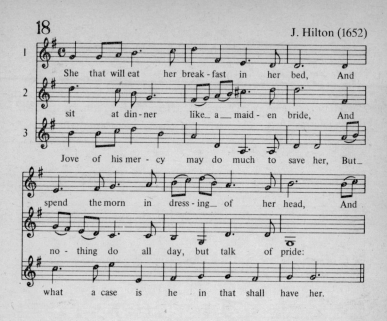

She that will eat her break-fast in her bed, And
sit at din-ner like_ a_ maid-en bride, And
Jove of his mer-cy may do much to save her, But_
spend the morn in dress-ing_ of her head, And
no-thing do all day, but talk of pride:
what a case is he in that shall have her.

19

J. Hilton (1652)

Here lies a wo-man, who can de-ny it, she
Her hus-band prays, if o'er her grave you walk, you
soft; for if she wakes, for if she wakes, she'll talk; tread
died in peace though lived un-qui-et.
would tread soft, you would tread
soft, for if she wakes, she'll talk.

20

J. Saville (1667)

Had she not care e-nough, care e-nough, care e-nough,

wed him, she fed him, and to the bed she led him, for

O how she nig-gled him, nig-gled him, nig-gled him!

had she not care e-nough of the old man? She

sev'n long win-ters she lif-ted him on; But

O how she nig-gled him all the night long!

21

E. Nelham (1667)

Hey down down down a-down, hey down down der-ry, Shall I

go with my true love now o-ver the fer-ry, And kiss her

ro-sy sweet lips un-til I am wea-ry, with a

22 Anon. (1667)

If day. If all be true as wo - men say, the__ night__ as __ good as is the

23 T. Brewer (1667)

Go, Da - mon, go, Am - a - ryl - lis bids a - dieu; Go

No, no, I care not for your pret - ty ar - bour nigh, Al -

Nor will I sit to hear you play, Nor

seek an - o - ther love, but prove to her more true.

-though great A - pol - lo can - not spy;

tune my__ voice to your roun - de - lay.

Note: The composer calls this 'The Answer' to Hilton's 'Turn Amaryllis to thy swain' (No. 16).

H. Purcell (1701)

25

H. Purcell (1701)

1. Once, twice, thrice I
2. since, and since I can no
3. so kiss my arse, so kiss my arse, so kiss my arse, dis-

Ju - - - - lia tried, the scorn - - - -
bet - ter, bet - ter thrive, I'll cringe
-dain - ful sow! Good cla - ret, good

- - ful puss as oft de - nied. And
to ne'er a bitch a - live. So kiss my arse,
cla - ret is my mis - tress now.

20

26

H. Purcell (1701)

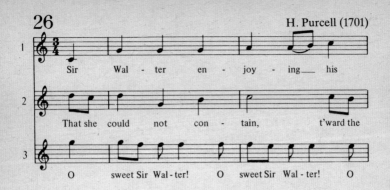

1. Sir Wal - ter en - joy - ing__ his

2. That she could not con - tain, t'ward the

3. O sweet Sir Wal - ter! O sweet Sir Wal - ter! O

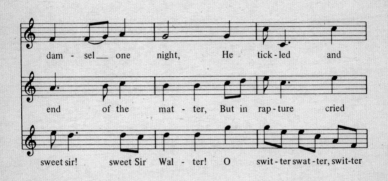

dam - sel__ one night, He tick - led and

end of the mat - ter, But in rap - ture cried

sweet sir! sweet Sir Wal - ter! O swit - ter swat - ter, swit - ter

pleas'd her to so great a de - light

out, O sweet Sir Wal - ter!

swat - ter, swit - ter swat - ter, swit - ter swat - ter, swit - ter swat - ter!

H. Purcell (1701)

28

H. Purcell (1685)

1. My wife has a tongue as good as e'er____
   twanged, At ev'ry word she bids me be hanged.

2. She's ug - ly, she's old and a curs - èd
   scold, With a dam - na-ble *num - quam sa - tis.*

3. For her tongue and her tail, if ev - er they
   fail, The de' il shall have her gra - tis.

29

M. Wise (1701)

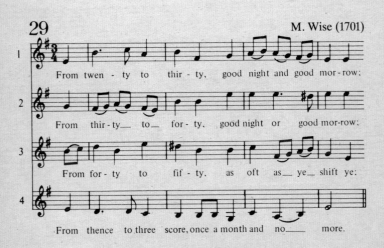

1. From twen - ty to thir - ty, good night and good mor - row;

2. From thir - ty__ to__ for - ty, good night or good mor-row;

3. From for - ty to fif - ty, as oft as__ ye__ shift ye;

4. From thence to three score, once a month and no____ more.

30   D. Lampe (1762)

1. Sit - ting by the fire,
2. Al - most starv'd with cold, For
3. want of fierce de - sire,____ I
4. heard a wo - man scold.

31   Anon. (1769a)

1. I love my Fan - ny with all my
2. - light and char - mer, guid - ed by____
3. hap - py I am, how dear thou

soul,   she is my heart's de - -

vir - tue which ne - ver fades; how

art,   I can't ex - press____ how

Note: When the first voice has sung the round three times, finish all together at 🕪

32

H. Harrington (1786a)

How great is the plea - sure, how

How great is the plea - sure, how

Sweet, sweet, how

sweet the de - light, when soft love and

sweet the de - light, when love, soft

sweet the de - light, when har - mo - ny, sweet

mu - sic to - ge - ther u - nite;

love, and mu - sic u - nite;

har - mo - ny and love do u - nite.

33

J. W. Callcott (1786)

Note: This round gained a prize medal in 1785 from the Nobleman's and Gentleman's Catch Club. The verb 'to Roger' is an eighteenth-century equivalent of the modern 'to have it off'. This round is another example of words from different sections combining to give a saucy meaning.

II   Wine, Ale and Song

34

Anon. (1609a)

1. Ban - bu - ry ale,

2. Where, where, where?

3. In the black - smith's house. I

4. would I were there.

35

Anon. (1611)

1. He that will an ale - house keep must

2. cham - ber and a feath - er bed, a

3. hey non - ny non - ny, hey non - ny no, hey

have three things in store: a

chim - ney and a hey non - ny non - ny,

non - ny no, hey__ non - ny no.

36 Anon. (1609a)

Now kiss the cup, cou - sin, with cour - te - sy,

And drink your part with a heart wil - ling - ly,

Then so shall we all a - gree mer - ri - ly.

37 Anon. (1609a)

Hey ho,

no - bo-dy at home,

Meat nor drink nor

mo - ney have I none.

Fill the pot, E - die.

Note: No. 38 following is the version of this round as it is widely sung today. It has been transformed to the more conventional three parts.

38

Anon.

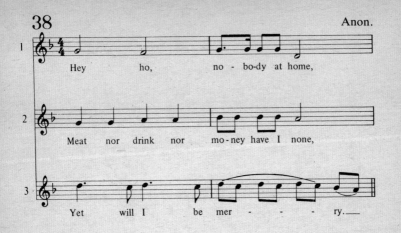

Hey ho, no-bo-dy at home,

Meat nor drink nor mo-ney have I none,

Yet will I be mer - - - ry.

39

Anon. (1609a)

Do - nec à boire

al - le bon com - pan - i -

- on, al - le - lu - ia,

al - le - lu - ia.

40 Anon. (1609a)

1. How should I sing well and not be wea - ry,

2. and not be wea - ry, since we lack mo - ney to

3. make us mer - ry, to make us mer - ry,

4. since we lack mo - ney to make us mer - ry,

5. since we lack mo - ney to make us mer - ry?

41 Anon. (1609a)

1. Sing you now af - ter me,

2. And as I sing, sing ye.

3. So shall we all a - gree,

4. Five parts in u - ni - ty.

5. Ding dong ding dong ding dong ding dong bell.

42 Anon. (1609a)

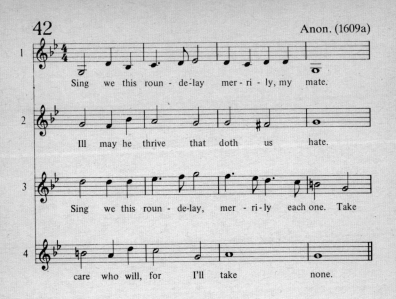

1. Sing we this roun - de-lay mer - ri - ly, my mate.

2. Ill may he thrive that doth us hate.

3. Sing we this roun - de-lay, mer - ri - ly each one. Take

4. care who will, for I'll take none.

43 Anon. (1609b)

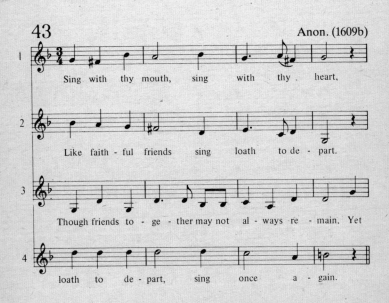

1. Sing with thy mouth, sing with thy heart,

2. Like faith - ful friends sing loath to de - part.

3. Though friends to - ge - ther may not al - ways re - main, Yet

4. loath to de - part, sing once a - gain.

44   Anon. (1609a)

1. To Ports - mouth, to Ports - mouth,

2. And there we will have a quart of wine,

3. The gal - lant ship the Mer - maid,

4. Did make us to spend there

it is a gal - lant town,

with a nut - meg brown did - dle down.

the li - on hang - ing stout,

our six - teen pence all out.

45

Anon. (1609a)

Sing we now mer - ri - ly, our
pur - ses be emp - ty, hey
ho! Let
them take care that list to spare, for
I will not do so.
Who can sing so
mer - ry a note as he that
can - not change a groat? Hey
ho, trol - ly lol - ly
lo, tro - lol - ly lo.

Anon. (1609a)

1. Come drink to me and
I will drink to thee,
And then shall
to thee,

2. I have lov'd the jol-ly tan-
kard full se-ven win-ters and
more. I lov'd it so long

3. He that loves not the tan-kard
is no ho-nest man, no
ho-nest man, And he is no right
honest man,

4. Tap the can-i-kin, toss the can-i-kin, troll the can-i-kin,
turn the can-i-kin, Hold, good son, and
fill us a fresh can,
That

we full well a - gree.

till that I went u - pon the score.

sol - dier that loves not the can.

we may quaff it round a - bout from man to man.

Note: Hilton (1652) attributed this round to William Byrd.

47 (𝄐) Anon. (1609a)

1. Hey down a - down, down a, be - hold and
three. 2. Take and fill this pot yet once a -
-gain. 3. Hey down a - down, down a, be - hold and
me.

see. Good host - ess, fill the pot for
-gain. We will for this time thus re -
see. This is the best ale, be - lieve

me, And yet it is the first of
- main. When this is spent fill pot a -
me. If ye will drink more then call

Note: Each voice should sing the three verses and end with 'me' at 𝄐

48

Anon. (1609a)

Go no more to Brain - ford un - less you love a
punk, for that wick - ed sin - ful town hath made
me drunk. Come fol - low me.

Note: In those days, 'punk' meant 'prostitute'.

49

J. Hilton (1652)

O ale *ab a - len - do,* thou li - quor of life,
But mine is too lit - tle to sound the least tit - tle
Al - though it will ne - ver be as big as I wish,

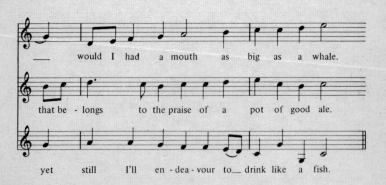

would I had a mouth as big as a whale.
that be - longs to the praise of a pot of good ale.
yet still I'll en - dea - vour to drink like a fish.

50

J. Hilton (1652)

1. Come fol - low, fol - low me, come

2. We'll each man take his cup, what-

3. Then let us mer - ry be, be

fol - low, fol - low me, And we will to the

-e - ver us be - fall, And we will drink all

mer - ry, my no - ble hearts, For a cup of old sher - ry will

ta - vern go with mirth and mer - ry glee.

up, all up, and for an - o - ther call.

make us mer - ry and we'll sing well our parts.

51   Anon. (1652)

1. Hey   we   to the o - ther world

2. Where 'tis thought they ve - ry mer - ry be;

3. There the man in the moon drinks cla - ret. A

4. health to you and me.

52   J. Hilton (1652)

1. Here is an old ground, here is an old ground.

2. Then hold it true, Dick, and sing your notes quick,

3. There-fore sing your notes quick, hold true your prick,

If right it be sung, 'twill prove a round.

quick, for you'll find a craf-ty trick.

then mer-ri-ly we will a - gree, three parts in u - ni - ty.

38

53

E. Nelham (1652)

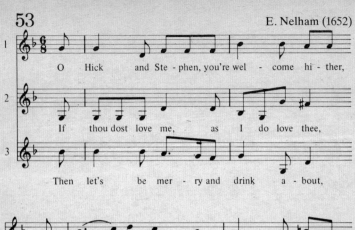

O Hick and Ste - phen, you're wel - come hi - ther,

If thou dost love me, as I do love thee,

Then let's be mer - ry and drink a - bout,

Let neigh - bours' chil - dren hold to - ge - ther.

How well shall we love one an - o - ther.

And ne - ver part till all be out.

54

J. Jenkins (1652)

A boat, a boat, haste to the fer - ry,

For we'll go o - ver to be mer - ry,

To laugh and sing and drink old sher - ry.

55

W. Lawes (1652)

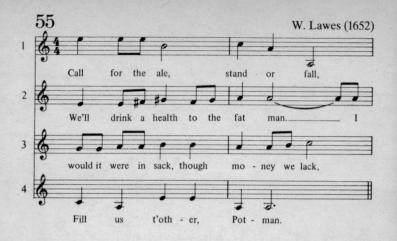

1. Call for the ale, stand or fall,

2. We'll drink a health to the fat man._____ I

3. would it were in sack, though mo - ney we lack,

4. Fill us t'oth - er, Pot - man.

56

W. Lawes (1652)

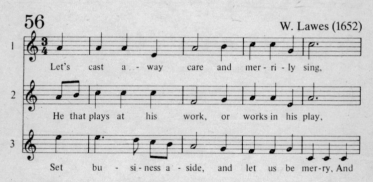

1. Let's cast a - way care and mer - ri - ly sing,

2. He that plays at his work, or works in his play,

3. Set bu - si - ness a - side, and let us be mer-ry, And

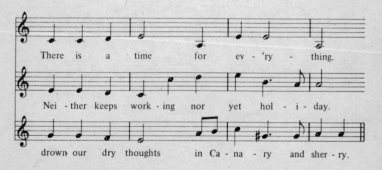

There is a time for ev - 'ry - thing.

Nei - ther keeps work - ing nor yet hol - i - day.

drown our dry thoughts in Ca - na - ry and sher - ry.

Note: Sack was a Spanish wine like sherry, both of which the English sweetened with sugar.
The Canary Islands supplied a richer version.

57

W. Lawes (1652)

1. Come quaff a-pace this brisk Ca-na-ry wine,____

2. ____ or fat Fa-ler-num shows;

3. -ses. Sink____ here all care, with

____ bet-ter then than the high,____

this who choo-ses, dips in the true,

mirth we'll fill____ the scene, and like mad Greek-ish

____ the high-prized Les-bian vine,____

true foun-tain____ of the____ Mu -

gods, piss____ *Min - ta-lyne.*

Note: See note to No. 56 for Canary wine. The rest are poetic references to ancient Roman vintages.

58

W. Lawes (1652)

Hang sor - row and cast a - way care, And

wine that makes the thoughts as - pire, And

_ and drink up all, _ The

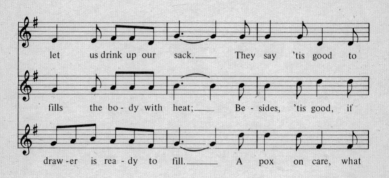

let us drink up our sack. _ They say 'tis good to

fills the bo - dy with heat; _ Be - sides, 'tis good, if

draw - er is rea - dy to fill. _ A pox on care, what

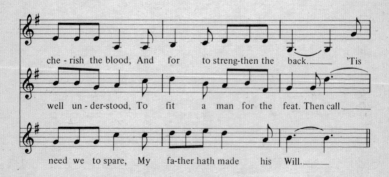

che - rish the blood, And for to streng-then the back. _ 'Tis

well un - der-stood, To fit a man for the feat. Then call _

need we to spare, My fa-ther hath made his Will. _

Note: His father, one thinks, has made his William Lawes.

59

W. Lawes (1667)

1. Come let us have a mer - ry heart, Our

2. The birds can sing with mer - ry glee, Not

3. Why should not we as mer - ry be, Con -

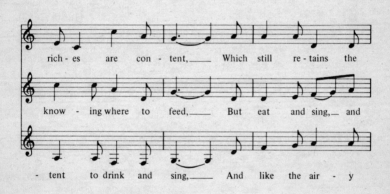

rich - es are con - tent,___ Which still re - tains the

know - ing where to feed,___ But eat and sing,___ and

- tent to drink and sing,___ And like the air - y

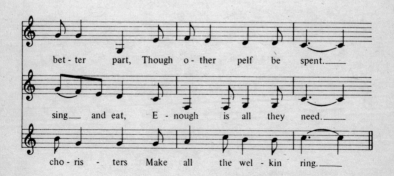

bet - ter part, Though o - ther pelf be spent.___

sing___ and eat, E - nough is all they need.___

cho - ris - ters Make all the wel - kin ring.___

43

60

H. Lawes (1652)

1. Now my lads, now my lads, now let's be mer - ry,

2. Here is old Cha - rin - go, ci - der and per - ry.

3. Then let us dance and sing, hey down down der - ry.

61

J. Hilton (1652)

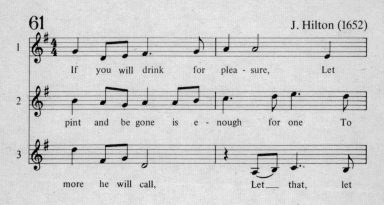

1. If you will drink for plea - sure, Let

2. pint and be gone is e - nough for one To

3. more he will call, Let that, let

each man take off his mea - sure. A

drink and pay of his trea - sure. But if

that man pay for all.

62

W. Lawes (1667)

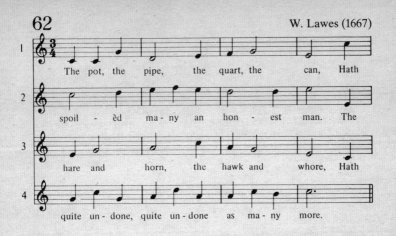

1. The pot, the pipe, the quart, the can, Hath

2. spoil - èd ma - ny an hon - est man. The

3. hare and horn, the hawk and whore, Hath

4. quite un - done, quite un - done as ma - ny more.

63

T. Brewer (1667)

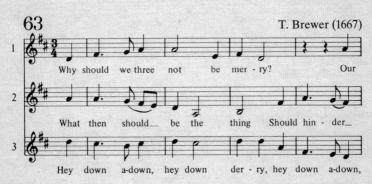

1. Why should we three not be mer - ry? Our

2. What then should__ be the thing Should hin - der__

3. Hey down a-down, hey down der - ry, hey down a-down,

ale is as brown as a ber - ry.

us to sing, hey down der - ry, down der - ry.

down a - down, down a - down, down der - ry.

64

1. This ale, my bon-ny lads, is as___
2. Here's to thee, lad. To my
3. Come to me, lad.

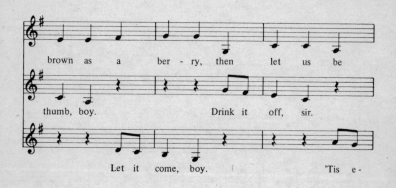

brown as a ber - ry, then let us be
thumb, boy. Drink it off, sir.
Let it come, boy. 'Tis e -

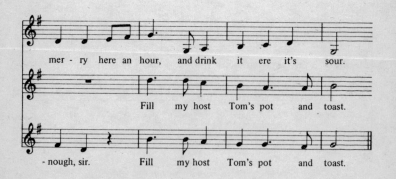

mer - ry here an hour, and drink it ere it's sour.
Fill my host Tom's pot and toast.
- nough, sir. Fill my host Tom's pot and toast.

65

G. Holmes (1667)

1. Eng - land, I do love thee dear - ly,
   Tho' thy li - quor be but wa - ter, hops and bar - ley.

2. France, thou af-ford'st us ac - tive spark-ling cla-ret, But I
   care not a pin, nor a but - ton for it.

3. Here's rich Ca - na - ry, you may pack and va - nish,
   For my mo - ney give me the old, old Span - ish.

Note: The 'old Spanish' would be a dry wine also known as 'sack' or 'sherry'. Rude remarks about claret were inspired equally by anti-French sentiment and by relatively high taxes imposed on imported French wines.

66

Anon. (1702)

1. Sing one, two, three,

2. Come fol - low me,

3. And so shall we

4. Good fel - lows___ be.

67

H. Purcell (1685)

1. Would you know how we meet o'er our

2. The sweet melts the sharp, the

3. We drink, laugh and gra - ti - fy

jol - ly full bowls, As we min - gle our

kind soothes the strong, And no - thing but

ev - 'ry de - sire; Love on - ly re -

li - quors, we min - gle our souls?

friend - ship grows all the night long.

- mains our un - quench - a - ble fire.

Note: Punch was usually served in bowls. A recipe of 1672 called for a quart of claret, half a pint of brandy, a little grated nutmeg, a little sugar and the juice of a lemon.

68

H. Purcell (1701)

1. If all be true that

2. — Good wine,

3. — Or a - ny

1. I do think, There are five rea - sons, there

2. a friend, or be - ing dry,

3. o - ther rea - son, or a - ny o - ther rea - son, or a - ny

1. are five rea - sons we should drink:—

2. Or lest we should be— by and— by,—

3. o - ther rea - son why, a - ny rea - son why.

69

H. Purcell (1701)

1. Now, now we are met, and hu - mours a-

2. Fill, fill it a - bout, to me let it

3. A health to the King, round, round, let it

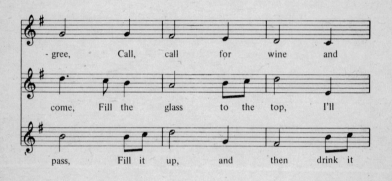

- gree, Call, call for wine and

come, Fill the glass to the top, I'll

pass, Fill it up, and then drink it

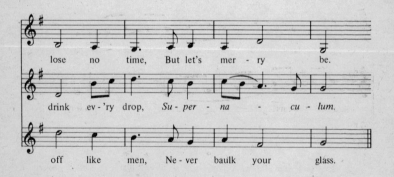

lose no time, But let's mer - ry be.

drink ev -'ry drop, *Su - per - na - cu - lum.*

off like men, Ne - ver baulk your glass.

50

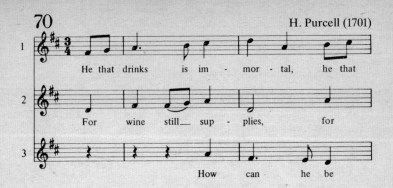

71

H. Purcell (1701)

1. Pale fa - ces stand by and our bright ones a - dore,
2. Come light up our pim - ples, all art we out - shine,
3. Clean glass - es are pen - cils, old cla - ret is oil;

We look like our wine, you worse than our score.

When the plump god does paint, each streak is div - ine.

He that sits for his pic - ture must sit a good while.

72

J. Clarke (1702)

1. In drink - ing full bum - pers there is no de - ceit,
2. Come, light all your pipes up, no sun do we need,
3. May our jol - ly club ne'er by in - tru - ders be broke,

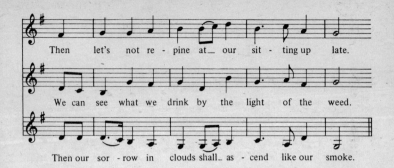

Then let's not re - pine at our sit - ting up late.

We can see what we drink by the light of the weed.

Then our sor - row in clouds shall as - cend like our smoke.

73

M. Wise (1731)

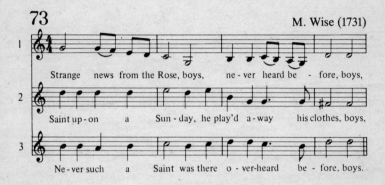

1 Strange news from the Rose, boys, ne - ver heard be - fore, boys,

2 Saint up - on a Sun - day, he play'd a - way his clothes, boys,

3 Ne - ver such a Saint was there o - ver-heard be - fore, boys.

74

E. Nelham (1762)

1 To - bac - co's but a va - pour,

2 And spends a great deal of pa - per;

3 But drink is a thing that doth com - fort a king

4 And makes an old crip - ple, makes an old crip-ple ca - per.

R. Brown (1731)

1. Of ho - nest malt li - quor let
2. But Lon - don - brew'd sta - ple, stout
3. To King, Lords and Com - mons, toast a

Eng - lish boys sing, A pox take French
Bur - ton and Lin - coln, They'd find us good
health ere we rise, Tho' we low - er our

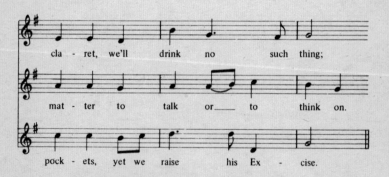

cla - ret, we'll drink no such thing;
mat - ter to talk or to think on.
pock - ets, yet we raise his Ex - cise.

Note: This catch is described as 'sung by three porters', presumably because the better-off by this time drank wine rather than beer. The excise tax on beer was introduced by the Parliamentarians in the Civil War conditions of 1643.

76

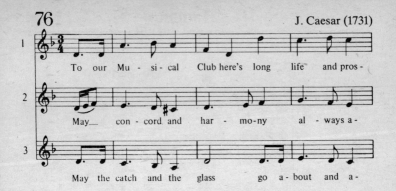

1. To our Mu - si - cal Club here's long life and pros -

2. May__ con - cord and har - mo - ny al - ways a -

3. May the catch and the glass go a - bout and a -

- pe - ri - ty, May it flou - - - - - -

- bound, And di - vi - - - - - -

- bout, And an - o - ther, and an - o - ther, and an -

- - rish with__ us and__ so__ on to pos - te - ri - ty. .

- - sions here on - ly in our mu - sic be found.

o - ther suc - ceed to the bot - tle that's out.

77 Anon. (1609a)

La - dy, come
down and see, the
cat sits in the
plum tree.

78 Anon. (1609a)

There lies a pud - ding in the fire and
— Whom should I call in? O
— Call in, call in, O

my part lies there - in, a.
thy good fel - lows and mine, a.
thy good fel - lows and mine, a.

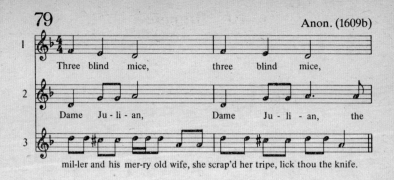

79   Anon. (1609b)

1. Three blind mice,   three blind mice,
2. Dame Ju - li - an,   Dame Ju - li - an, the
3. mil-ler and his mer-ry old wife, she scrap'd her tripe, lick thou the knife.

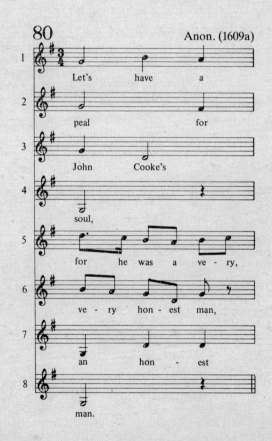

80   Anon. (1609a)

1. Let's have a
2. peal for
3. John Cooke's
4. soul,
5. for he was a ve - ry,
6. ve - ry hon - est man,
7. an hon - est
8. man.

81 Anon. (1609a)

1. Jin - kin the Jes - ter was wont to make glee With

2. Jar - vis the Jug - gler till an - gry was he. Then

3. Wil - kin the Wise - man did wise - ly fore - see, That

4. Jug - gler and Jes - ter should gent - ly a - gree.

5. Hey down down, down down, der-ry down down, der-ry down down.

82 Anon. (1609a)

1. Jack boy, ho, boy, news.

2. The cat is in the well,

3. Let us ring now for her knell,

4. Ding dong ding dong bell.

83   Anon. (1609b)

1. Hold thy peace, and I pri-thee hold thy peace,

2. thou knave, hold thy peace, thou knave,

3. thou knave.

84   Anon. (1609b)

1. I C U B A K,

2. And ev - er - more will be,

3. Though John Cooke he saith nay,

4. O, what a knave is he.

85   Anon. (1609a)

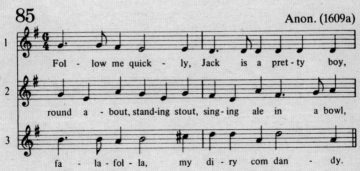

1. Fol - low me quick - ly, Jack is a pret - ty boy,

2. round a - bout, stand-ing stout, sing-ing ale in a bowl,

3. fa - la-fol - la, my di - ry com dan - dy.

86   Anon. (1609b)

1. The maid she went a - milk - ing

2. All in a mis - ty morn - ing.

3. — Down fell her milk - ing pail, —

4. — Up went her did - dle did - dle tail.

87   Anon. (1611)

1. My mis - tress will not be con - tent To

2. But fol - lowing still the wo - man's fash - ion, Al -

3. For with the word she'd not dis - pense, And

take a jest, a jest, a jest, as Chau - cer meant;

-lows it, al - lows it for the new trans - la - tion;

yet, and yet, and yet, and yet I know she loves the sense.

88

J. Hilton (1652)

Come fol - low, fol - low, fol - low,

Whi - ther shall I fol - low, fol - low, fol - low,

To the gal - low, to the gal - low,

fol - low, fol - low, fol - low me.

whi - ther shall I fol - low, fol - low thee?

to_____ the gal - low, gal - low tree.

89

E. Nelham (1652)

Cuc - koo, go neigh - bours help us to

hedge in the cuc - koo, keep, keep,

keep, O keep in the cuc - koo.

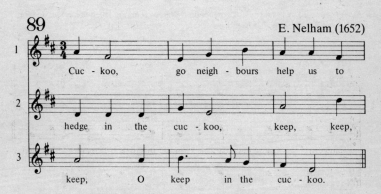

Note: This is a version of a traditional folk tale, always told of a neighbouring village, in which the stupid inhabitants believe that if they can keep the cuckoo from migrating, they will have spring all year round.

90

T. Holmes (1652)

This gear goes____ hard, 'tis al -
- most marred, 'tis ____ driv'n so ____ like a cart.

'Tis good in sight, then
sing it right, or else you lose the o - ther quart.

I'll ne'er go out, but sing it
right, three times a - bout, and friend - ly part.

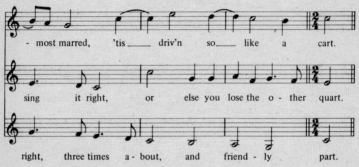

Note: Impressed by the ingenious syncopation, Warren (1763) reissued this round, in score, to the words 'This song goes hard'.

91

J. Hilton (1652)

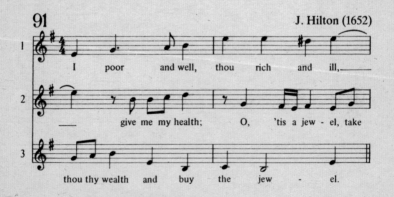

I poor and well, thou rich and ill, ____
____ give me my health; O, 'tis a jew - el, take
thou thy wealth and buy the jew - el.

92

E. Nelham (1652)

1. Wilt thou lend me thy mare to ride a mile? No,_____
   ____ she's lame go-ing o - - ver a stile.____

2. ____ But if thou wilt her to me____ spare,
   thou shalt have mon - ey for thy mare.

3. O,_____ say you so, say you so, mon-ey will
   make my mare to go, mon - ey will make my mare to go?

93

W. Lawes (1652)

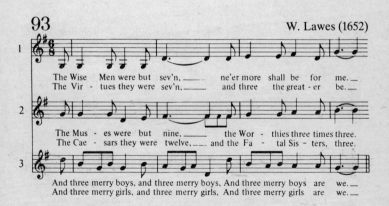

1. The Wise Men were but sev'n,_____ ne'er more shall be for me.____
   The Vir - tues they were sev'n,_____ and three the great - er be.____

2. The Mus - es were but nine,_____ the Wor - thies three times three.
   The Cae - sars they were twelve,____ and the Fa - tal Sis - ters, three.

3. And three merry boys, and three merry boys, And three merry boys are we.____
   And three merry girls, and three merry girls, And three merry girls are we.____

Note: The 'three merry boys' were probably William Lawes, his brother Henry and John Wilson, another musician.

94

J. Hilton (1652)

Let Si - mon's beard a -
'Tis no dis - grace to
Then mock not, nor scoff not, nor

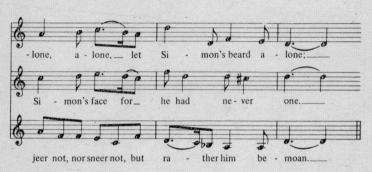

- lone, a - lone, __ let Si - mon's beard a - lone; __
Si - mon's face for __ he had ne - ver one. __
jeer not, nor sneer not, but ra - ther him be - moan. __

95

J. Hilton (1667)

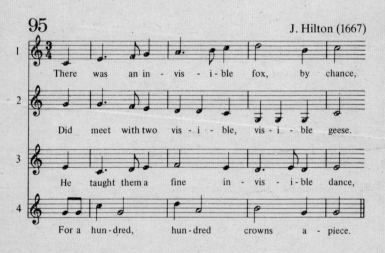

There was an in - vis - i - ble fox, by chance,
Did meet with two vis - i - ble, vis - i - ble geese.
He taught them a fine in - vis - i - ble dance,
For a hun - dred, hun - dred crowns a - piece.

96

M. White (1667)

1. My dame has a lame, tame crane.

2. My dame has a crane that is lame.

3. Good gen-tle Jane, let my dame's lame, tame

4. crane Feed and come home a - gain.

97

H. Purcell (1686)

1. Un - der this stone lies Ga - bri-el John, In the
    year of Our Lord one thou - sand and one.

2. Co - ver his__ head with turf__ or stone, 'Tis all
    one, 'tis all one, with turf or stone, 'tis all one.

3. Pray for the soul of gen - tle__ John, If you
    please, you may, or let__ it a - lone, 'tis all one.

W. Lawes (1667)

1. Come Am - a - ryl - lis, now let us be mer - ry, Sing
2. Da - mon takes joy in his trea - sure, his trea - sure, And
3. Ploughs would stand still, the world would soon per - ish, For

no - li - fi, to - li - fi, to - li - fi, cher - ry. Let
Ti - terus in pip - ing and danc - ing takes plea - sure; And
thee and thy Phyl - lis there's no man would che - rish, And

Phyl - lis thy sis - ter, as brown as a ber - ry, Sing
no man can e - ver be heart - i - ly mer - ry, But
shep - herds would of their flocks quick - ly be wea - ry, But

no - li - fi, to - li - fi, to - li - fi, cher - ry.
no - li - fi, to - li - fi, to - li - fi, cher - ry.
no - li - fi, to - li - fi, to - li - fi, cher - ry.

W. Lawes (1652)

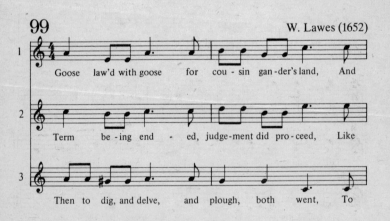

Goose law'd with goose for cou - sin gan - der's land, And

Term be - ing end - ed, judge - ment did pro - ceed, Like

Then to dig, and delve, and plough, both went, To

fox, the law - yer, took the case in hand.

fools they met, and beg - gars they a - greed.

get by pain what id - ly they had spent.

100
E. Nelham (1667)

1 Slaves to the world should be toss'd in a blan - ket,

2 Like to the wheel that's turn - ing up so

3 down a - gain and down a - gain, the

if I might have my will,

fast on yon - der hill, And falls_____

ground it touch un - til.

101

H. Purcell (1686)

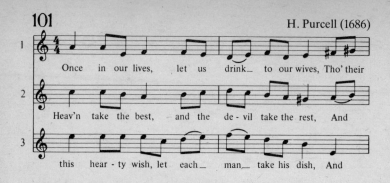

1. Once in our lives, let us drink to our wives, Tho' their

2. Heav'n take the best, and the de-vil take the rest, And

3. this hear-ty wish, let each man take his dish, And

num - bers be but small.

so we shall get rid of them all. To

drink, drink till he fall.

102

H. Purcell (1685)

1. 'Tis wo - men make us love,

2. 'Tis love that makes us sad,

3. 'Tis sad - ness makes us drink,

4. And drink - ing makes us mad.

H. Purcell (1701)

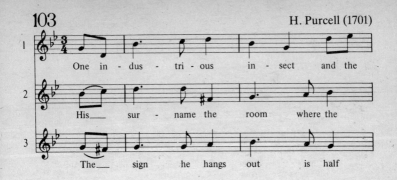

1 One in - dus - tri - ous in - sect and the

2 His___ sur - name the room where the

3 The___ sign he hangs out is half

sweet - ness of___ th'o - ther Is the Chris - ti - an

fire's in the mid - dle And___ some say he

fish and half flesh, And he sells as true___

name of our well___ be - lov'd bro - ther.

plays _____ ve - ry well on the___ fid - dle.

wine as good fel - low can wish.

Note: This is 'a *rebus* upon Mr Anthony Hall, who keeps the Maremaid Tavern in Oxford and plays his part very well on the violin. The words are by Mr Tomlinson.'

104

H. Purcell (1686)

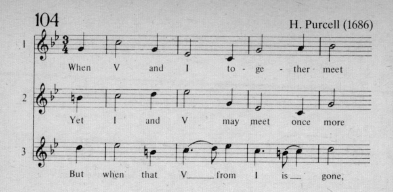

1. When V and I to-ge-ther meet
2. Yet I and V may meet once more
3. But when that V___ from I is___ gone,

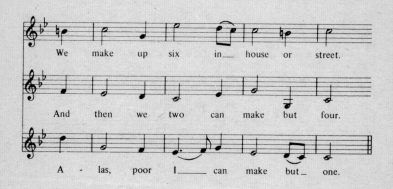

We make up six in___ house or street.
And then we two can make but four.
A - las, poor I___ can make but___ one.

105

H. Purcell (1685)

1. To thee, to thee, and to a maid That
2. And laugh___ and sing and kiss and play, And
3. Such, such a lass, kind friend, and drink - ing,

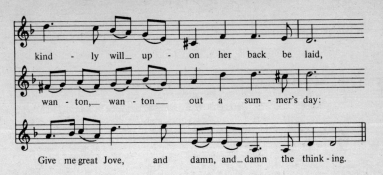

107

H. Purcell (1701)

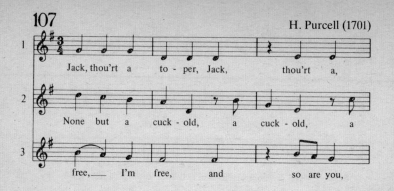

ring, ring, ring, ring, we're so so - ber, so

com-ing, com-ing, com-ing, com-ing, com-ing, com-ing late,

bold - ly, knock bold - ly, tho' watch-men cry

so - ber, so so - ber, 'twere a shame___ to part.

fears a dom - es - - - - - tic strife. I'm

'Past_____ two o' - clock'.

108

Anon. (1701)

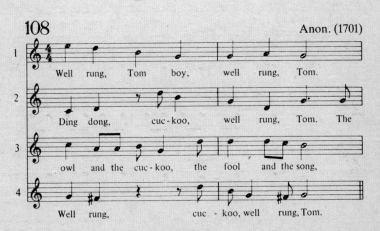

1. Well rung, Tom boy, well rung, Tom.

2. Ding dong, cuc - koo, well rung, Tom. The

3. owl and the cuc - koo, the fool and the song,

4. Well rung, cuc - koo, well rung, Tom.

109

I. Lenton (1701)

1. The mate to a cock, and corn tall as wheat,
2. His sur-name be - gins with the grace of a cat,
3. His skill and per - for - mance each au - di - tor wins, But

Is his Chris - tian name who in mu - sic's com - plete.

And con-cludes with the house of a her - mit, note that.

the po - et de - serves a good kick on the shins.

Note: This is 'a *rebus* on the late Mr Henry Purcell's name, by Mr Tomlinson'.

110

R. Brown (1701)

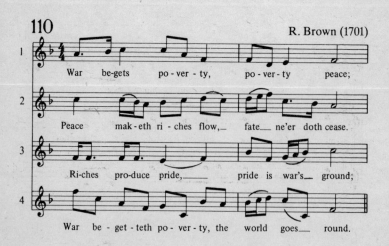

1. War be-gets po - ver - ty, po - ver - ty peace;
2. Peace mak - eth ri - ches flow, fate ne'er doth cease.
3. Ri - ches pro - duce pride, pride is war's ground;
4. War be - get - teth po - ver - ty, the world goes round.

111

R. Brown (1731)

We cats when as-sem-bled at mid-night to-ge-ther, For

If dogs be in ken-nel, all fast__ in their straw, We

But if they sur-prise us, and put us to__ flight, We

in - no-cent pur - ring, pur - ring, for in - no-cent

march, and we miaow, mi - - aow,

fret, fret, and we spit, fret, spit, spit, give a squall,

pur - ring, pur - ring, in moon - shi - ny wea - ther,

mi - aow, with-out scratch or a claw;

squall,_____ and good-night.

112

J. Isum (1731)

1. When Celia was learning on the spinet to play, Her tutor stood by her to show her, to show her, to show her the way.

2. She shook not the note, which angered him much, And made him, and made him cry 'Zounds, 'tis a long prick, a long prick, a long pricked note you touch.'

3. Surprised was the lady to hear him complain, And said, and said, and said, 'I will shake it, I will shake it when I come to't again.'

Note: The young lady was learning to play the clavichord, not the spinet; it is the only keyboard instrument where a note can be sustained with a vibrato effect by rocking the finger on the key.

Anon. (1762)

114

Anon. (1731)

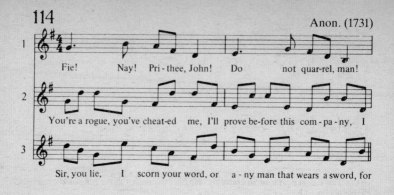

1. Fie! Nay! Pri-thee, John! Do not quar-rel, man!

2. You're a rogue, you've cheat-ed me, I'll prove be-fore this com-pa-ny, I

3. Sir, you lie, I scorn your word, or a-ny man that wears a sword, for

Let's be mer-ry and drink a - bout.

caren't a far-thing, sir, for all you are so stout.

all you huff, who cares a turd or who cares for you?

115

R. Brown (1731)

1. En-tombed here lies good Sir Har-ry, be-

2. When he did live and had his feel - ing.

3. But now he's dead and lost his feel - ing,

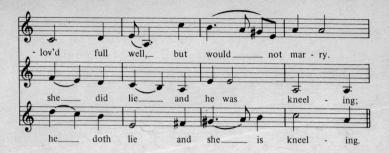

-lov'd   full   well,__   but   would____   not   mar - ry.

she__   did   lie____   and   he was   kneel - ing;

he__   doth   lie   and   she__   is   kneel - ing.

Note: This is 'an epitaph on Sir Harry — and his mistress: his statue lying on the tomb and hers kneeling at his feet'.

116

T. Warren (1763b)

Here   stand   I   for

cast   a   scorn - ful   eye   on,   to

each   whore   here   be

soon   want   one   to   lie   on,   you'd

whores   as   great   To

cast   a   scorn - ful   eye   on.   Should

doomed   a   sheet,   You'd

soon   want   one   to   lie   on.

Note: According to Warren, the words of this round 'were pinned to a sheet in which a woman stood to do penance in the church'.

117

G. Berg (1766)

1. Fair Urs - ley in a___ mer - ry mood con -

2. Quoth Wood - ward, if my___ judge - ment's right, and

3. Quoth Urs - ley, then for plea - sure's sake, each

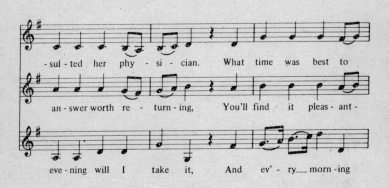

-sul - ted her phy - si - cian. What time was best to

an - swer worth re - turn - ing, You'll find it pleas - ant-

eve - ning will I take it, And ev' - ry___ morn - ing

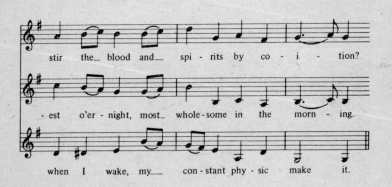

stir the___ blood and___ spi - rits by co - i - tion?

- est o'er - night, most___ whole - some in the morn - ing.

when I wake, my___ con - stant phy - sic make it.

118

C. Burney (1769a)

1. Mor - tals, learn your lives___ to mea - sure,
2. Soon your spring must have a fall,
3. Then you'll ask, but none___ will give,

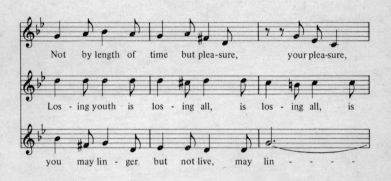

1. Not by length of time but plea-sure, your plea-sure,
2. Los - ing youth is los - ing all, is los - ing all, is
3. you may lin - ger but not live, may lin - - -

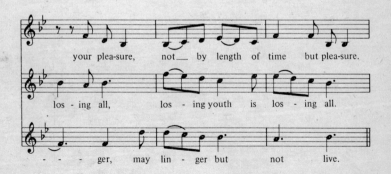

1. your plea-sure, not___ by length of time but plea-sure.
2. los - ing all, los - ing youth is los - ing all.
3. - - - ger, may lin - ger but not live.

119

Anon. (thirteenth century)

1 Sum - mer is a - com - ing in,_____

2 Loud - ly sing, cuc - koo.

3 Grow - eth seed and blow - eth mead And

4 springs the wood a - new.

5 Sing cuc - koo.

6 Ewe now bleat - eth af - ter lamb, Low - eth

7 af - ter calf the cow.

8 Bul - lock start - eth, buck now vert - eth,

9 Mer - ry sing cuc - koo.

10 Cuc - koo, cuc - koo,_____

GROUND

Note: Although this round could, in principle, be sung by twelve voices (or by fourteen, counting the two singing the ground), the original instructions read 'Four companions can sing this rota. But it ought not to be rendered by fewer than three, or two at the least, in addition to those who sing the bass.' (Translation given in *Grove's Dictionary of Music*, 5th edition.)

For the original words, see the *Oxford Book of English Verse*.

120

Anon. (1609a)

121   Anon. (1609a)

1. Blow thy horn, thou jol-ly hun-ter, thy hound for to re-vive, a.

2. Show thy-self a good hunts-man whilst that thou art a-live, a, that

3. men may say and sing with thee, thou hast a mer-ry life, a;

4. In plea-sure all the day, and Ve-nus mate to wife, a.

122   Anon. (1609a)

1. The night-in-gale, the mer-ry night-in-gale,

2. The pret-ty nim-ble doe doth trip it to and fro,

3. The cuc-koo he doth fly from tree to tree,

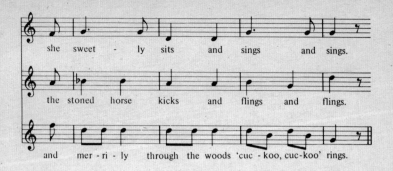

she sweet - ly sits and sings and sings.

the stoned horse kicks and flings and flings.

and mer - ri - ly through the woods 'cuc - koo, cuc - koo' rings.

123   Anon. (1611)

1 And seest thou my cow 'to-day, fow - ler?

2 The bells ring in to Ma - tins,

3 Bim bom bim bom - a - bom bom.

And seest thou my cow to-day, fow - ler?

the bells ring in to Ma - tins:

Bim bom bim bom - a - bom bom.

Anon. (1609a)

1. Jol - ly shep - herd and up - on a hill as he sat, so loud he blew his lit - tle horn, and kept right well his gate.

2. Ear - ly in a morn - ing, late in an eve - ning, and ev - er blew this lit - tle boy, so mer - ri - ly pip - ing.

3. Ter - li ter - lo, ter - li ter - lo, ter - li ter - lo ter - li, ter - li ter - lo, ter - li ter - lo, ter - li ter - lo ter - li.

125

Anon. (1609a)

1. Now Rob-in lend to me thy bow,

Sweet Rob - in lend to me thy bow,

For I must now a - hunt - ing with my la - dy go,

With my sweet la - dy go.

2. And whither will thy lady go?
   Sweet Wilkin, tell it unto me:
   And thou shalt have my hawk, my hound and eke my bow,
   To wait on thy lady.

3. My lady will to Uppingham,
   To Uppingham forsooth will she,
   And I myself appointed for to be the man,
   To wait on my lady.

4. Adieu, good Wilkin, all beshrewd,
   Thy hunting nothing pleaseth me,
   But yet beware thy babbling hounds stray not abroad,
   For ang'ring of thy lady.

5. My hounds shall be led in the line,
   So well I can assure it thee:
   Unless by view of strain some pursue I may find,
   To please my sweet lady.

6. With that the lady she came in,
   And willed them all for to agree:
   For honest hunting never was accounted sin,
   Nor never shall for me.

126   J. Hilton (1652)

1. The pret - ty lark, climb - ing the wel - kin

2. ——— peer, I near my deer, then——

3. a - dieu, she saith, a - dieu deer,

clear, chants with a cheer, heer,——

fall - ing thence, her fall she seems to rue;

deer a - dieu, a - dieu.

127   M. White (1667)

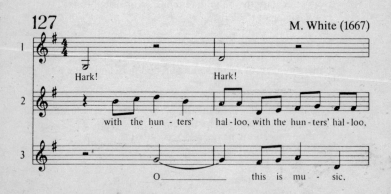

Hark!   Hark!

with the hun - ters' hal - loo, with the hun - ters' hal - loo,

O——— this is mu - sic,

Hark, how the woods do ring

and the cry that they fol - low, that they fol - low.

this is mu - sic for a king.

128

J. Hilton (1652)

1. What shall he have that kill'd the deer?

2. Take you no scorn to wear a horn,

3. Thy fa - ther's fa - ther bore it

4. The horn, the horn, the lus - ty horn

His lea - ther skin and horns to wear.

It was a crest ere thou wast born.

And thy fa - ther wore it.

Is not a thing to laugh to scorn.

129

E. Nelham (1652)

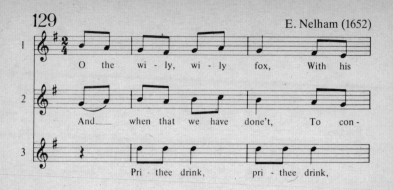

1. O the wi - ly, wi - ly fox, With his

2. And___ when that we have done't, To con-

3. Pri - thee drink, pri - thee drink,

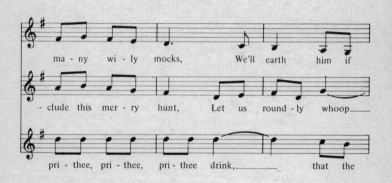

ma - ny wi - ly mocks, We'll earth him if

- clude this mer - ry hunt, Let us round - ly whoop___

pri - thee, pri - thee, pri - thee drink,___ that the

you'll but fol - low.___

___ and hol - low.___

hun - ters may fol - low.___

130

L. Atterbury (1766)

1. With horns and hounds in— cho-rus let's
2. The— sport's ex-ceed-ing glo-rious, a-
3. Now the stag— is— rous'd be-fore us, a-

ush-er in the day, with horns, with
rise, make no de-lay, a-rise, a-rise,
-way, come, come a-way, come a-way, come a-way, the—

hounds, let's— ush-er— in the day.——
a-rise, a-rise, make no de-lay.
stag is— rous'd, a-way, come, come a-way.——

131

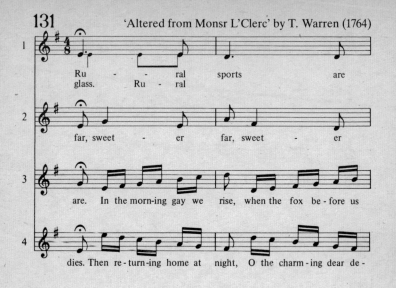

Note: When the first person has sung the round three times he is to finish with the word 'glass', all voices finishing at ⌢ with him.

132

J. B. Marella (1764)

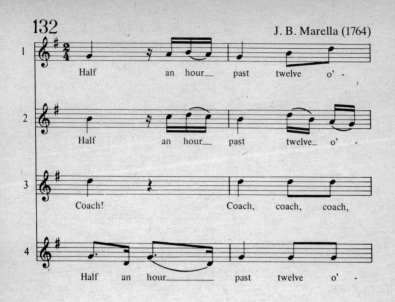

1. Half an hour past twelve o' -

2. Half an hour past twelve o' -

3. Coach! Coach, coach, coach,

4. Half an hour past twelve o' -

clock, star - light morn - ing.

clock, star - light morn - ing.

coach! Coach! Coach, coach!

clock, star - light morn - ing.

133

Anon. (1609a)

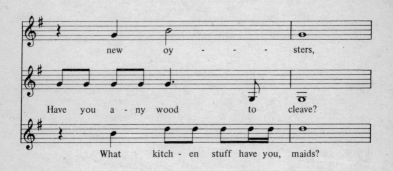

134

Anon. (1609b)

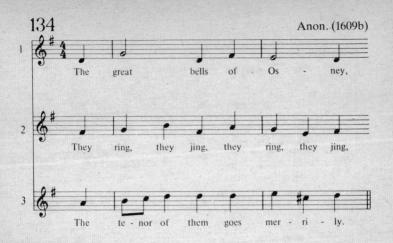

1. The great bells of Os - ney,

2. They ring, they jing, they ring, they jing,

3. The te - nor of them goes mer - ri - ly.

135

M. White (1667)

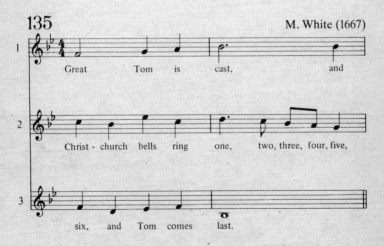

1. Great Tom is cast, and

2. Christ - church bells ring one, two, three, four, five,

3. six, and Tom comes last.

Note: At the Dissolution, the bells from Osney Abbey went to Christchurch Cathedral at Oxford. There Great Tom still chimes 101 strokes (one for each of the original scholars of the college) at five past nine each evening. (See also Nos. 134 and 136.)

136

H. Aldrich (1701)

1. Hark, the bon - ny Christ - church bells, one,

2. Hark, the first and se - cond bell, that

3. Tin - gle tin - gle ting, goes the small bell at nine, to

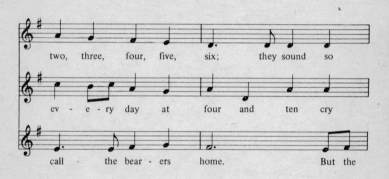

two, three, four, five, six; they sound so

ev - e - ry day at four and ten cry

call the bear - ers home. But the

woun - dy great, so wond - 'rous sweet, and they

come, come, come, come, come to pray'rs, and the

de'il a man will leave his can till he

troll   so   mer - ri - ly,   mer - ri - ly.

ver - ger   troops   be - fore   the   deer.

hears   the   might - y   Tom!

137
Anon. (1667)

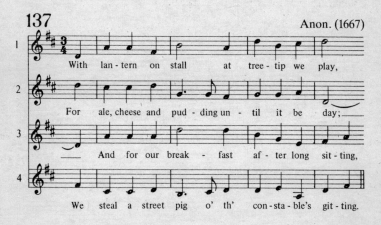

1 With lan - tern on stall   at tree - tip we play,

2 For ale, cheese and pud - ding un - til it be day;

3 ____ And for our break - fast af - ter long sit - ting,

4 We steal a street pig o' th' con - sta - ble's git - ting.

Note: This is called 'The Watchman's Catch'. In London as late as the nineteenth century, the watch consisted of old men who sat up all night in their portable shelters, with a rattle to give the alarm.

138
Anon. (1762)

1 Row   the boat,   Whit - ting - ton,

2 Thou   wor - thy   cit - i - zen,

3 Lord   Mayor   of   Lon - don.

139

T. Arne (1763a)

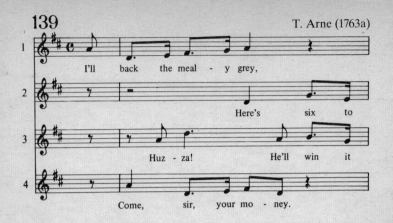

1. I'll back the meal - y grey,
2. Here's six to
3. Huz - za! He'll win it
4. Come, sir, your mo - ney.

the meal - y grey, I'll back the meal - y grey, for
four, six to four, I'll bet you two to one, I'll
still. I'll take the red, I'll take the
What! You did not lay? Bas - ket him,

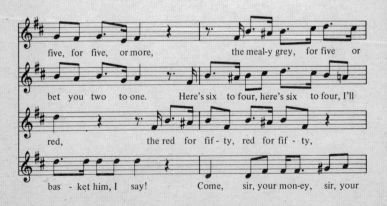

five, for five, or more, the meal - y grey, for five or
bet you two to one. Here's six to four, here's six to four, I'll
red, the red for fif - ty, red for fif - ty,
bas - ket him, I say! Come, sir, your mon - ey, sir, your

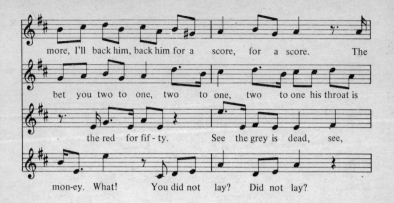

more, I'll back him, back him for a score, for a score. The
bet you two to one, two to one, two to one his throat is
the red for fif-ty. See the grey is dead, see,
mon-ey. What! You did not lay? Did not lay?

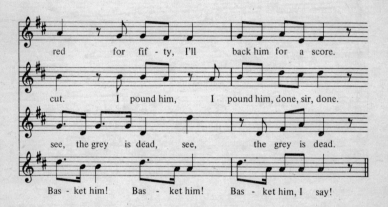

red for fif-ty, I'll back him for a score.
cut. I pound him, I pound him, done, sir, done.
see, the grey is dead, see, the grey is dead.
Bas-ket him! Bas-ket him! Bas-ket him, I say!

Note: Arne titles this 'The Cockfight'. Heavy betting was an essential part of this sport.

140

J. Blow (1731)

1. Here are the rar - i - ties of the whole fair: Pim - per - le - pimp and the wise danc - ing mare; Here's raff - ling, a pox take the Mayor!

2. val - iant St George and the Dra - gon, a farce, A girl of fif - teen with strange moles on her arse.

3. Here is Vi - en - na be - sieged, a rare thing; And here's Punch - in - el - lo, shown thrice to the King.

4. La - dies masked to the clois - ters re - pair; But there will be no

141

W. Hayes (1786a)

1 Chairs to mend, old chairs to mend,

2 mack - er - el, new mack - er - el,

3 Old rags, a - ny old rags, take

rush or cane bot - tom'd old chairs to mend, old

new mack - er - el, new

mon - ey for your old rags; a - ny hare skins or

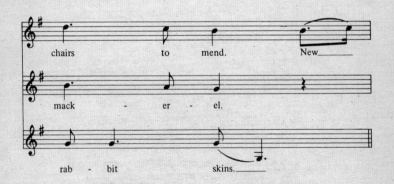

chairs to mend. New_____

mack - er - el.

rab - bit skins._____

Note: These are described as 'Three Oxford Cries'.

142   Anon. (1609a)

All in - to ser - vice, let us ring mer - ri - ly to - ge - ther, ding dong ding dong bell.

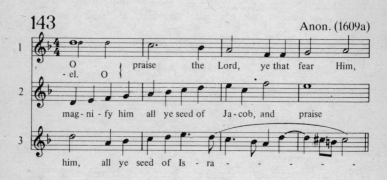

143   Anon. (1609a)

- el. O praise the Lord, ye that fear Him, mag - ni - fy him all ye seed of Ja - cob, and praise him, all ye seed of Is - ra - el.

144   Anon. (1609a)

A - diu - va - nos De - us.

145

Anon. (1609a)

Mi - se - re - re nos - tri, Do - mi - ne, se - cun - dum mi - se - ri - cor - di - am tu - am.

146

Anon. (1609a)

O my fear - ful dreams, ne - ver for - get shall I: me - thought I - demned to die, whose name was Je -

I, ne - ver for - get shall heard a mai - den's child con - sus, whose name was Je - sus.

147

Anon. (1609a)

Joy in the
gates of
Je - ru -
- sa - lem.
Peace be in
Zi - on.

148

Anon. (1609a)

1. O Lord on whom I do de - pend,
2. Thou seest my sor - rows what they are,
3. But on - ly Thou whose aid I crave,

Be - hold my care - ful heart;
My grief is known to Thee;
Whose mer - cy still is prest,

And when Thy will and plea - sure is,
And there is none that can re - move,
To ease all those that come to Thee

Re - lease me of my smart.
Or take the same from me.
For suc - cour and for rest.

149

J. Hilton (1652)

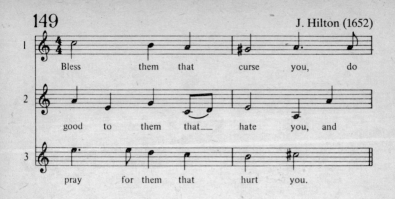

Bless them that curse you, do
good to them that__ hate you, and
pray for them that hurt you.

150

J. Hilton (1652)

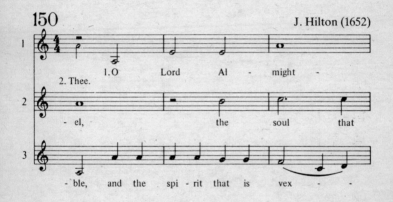

1. O Lord Al - might -
2. Thee.
- el, the soul that
- ble, and the spi - rit that is vex - -

- y, O God of Is - - ra -
is in__ trou - - - - -
- ed, cri - - eth un - - to__

151

J. Cobb (1652)

1. Hal - le - lu - ia, hal - -

2. - ia.

- le - lu - ia, hal - le -

- lu - ia, hal - le - lu - -

152

W. Lawes (1652)

Wars are our de-light, we

drink as we fight,

ta - ra - ra ra ra,

dub - a - dub dub - a - dub dub,

bounce,

tan ta - ra ran tan tan.

W. Lawes (1667)

Come fol - low me, brave hearts, and stout -

Keep your ranks and stand your ground; let the

- dub' beat; and if we give the foil, and

- ly play your parts; sound out the

trum - pets brave - ly sound,

if we give the foil, sound out the

trum - pet, sound out the trum - pet, sound out the

brave - - - - - ly

trum - pet, sound out the trum - pet, sound out the

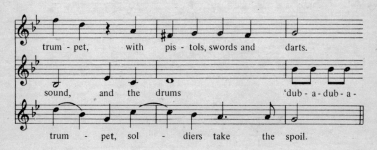

trum - pet, with pis - tols, swords and darts.

sound, and the drums 'dub - a - dub - a -

trum - pet, sol - diers take the spoil.

154

1. Is Char - le - roi's siege come, come, come to?

2. Then charge_____ all your guns, boys, as

3. Let en - gin - eer Vau - ban shoot the de - vil, the

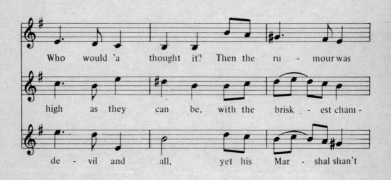

Who would 'a thought it? Then the ru - mour was

high as they can be, with the brisk - est cham -

de - vil and all, yet his Mar - shal shan't

false, was false, false,

- pagne rammed_____ down, rammed_____ down, down, down,

dance,_____ no,__ no, no, no, shan't

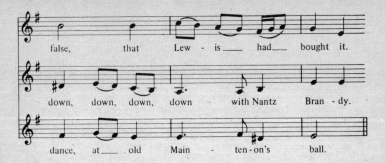

false, that Lew - is ___ had ___ bought it.

down, down, down, down with Nantz Bran - dy.

dance, at ___ old Main - ten - on's ball.

Note: This refers to a minor attempt on Charleroi by the French army in 1692. A year later they besieged it successfully, after defeating King William's Anglo-Dutch army at Landon.

155

H. Carey (1786a)

1. Curst be the wretch that's bought and sold, And

2. For when e - lec - tion is not free, In

3. And he who sells his sin - gle right Would

bar - ters ___ lib - er - ty for gold;

vain we boast of lib - er - ty.

sell his ___ coun - try if he might.

156

H. Purcell (1685)

God save our sov'-reign Charles, our faith's de-fen-der.

Pro-tect Queen Cath'-rine, Eng-land's nurs-ing mo-ther.

Who to his pi-ous votes de-nies his hand –

Let all good men his laws and hon-our ten-der.

Pre-serve York's Duke, our King's il-lus-trious bro-ther,

I pray for him too, but wish him out o'th' land.

157

Boyce (1763b)

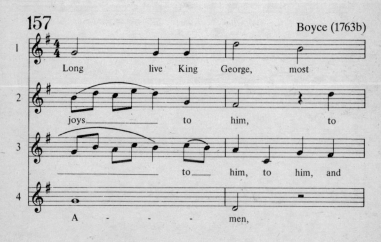

Long live King George, most

joys to him, to

to him, to him, and

A - - - men,

happy, happy days to see. All

him and his pos - te - ri - ty, all joys

his pos - te - ri - ty.

a - men, a - men.

158

Anon. (1762)

1. Long live our King and may all grace at -
2. May all their ef - forts prove in vain who
3. Then peace and plen - ty hand in hand shall

- tend his great and roy - al race.

would an - noy his glo - rious reign.

join to bless this hap - py land.

VII Laments

Anon. (1609a)

159

Love, love, sweet
thee, for For - tune hath de -
For - tune my foe_____ most con -
- ry; but yet my love, my sweet love, fare -

love, for e - ver - more fare - well to
- ceiv - èd me, de - ceiv - èd me.
- tra - ry hath wrought_____ me this mi - se -
- well to thee, fare - well to thee.

160

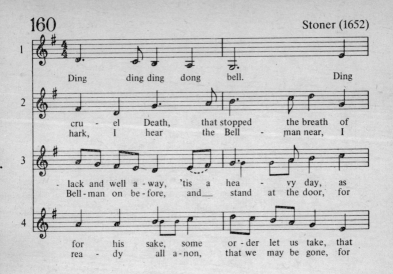

1. Ding ding ding dong bell. Ding

2. cru - el Death, that stopped the breath of
   hark, I hear the Bell - man near, I

3. - lack and well a - way, 'tis a hea - vy day, as
   Bell - man on be - fore, and stand at the door, for

4. for his sake, some or - der let us take, that
   rea - dy all a - non, that we may be gone, for

ding ding ding dong bell. { 1. O
                             { 2. Hark,

him I lov'd so well. A -
hear the bell come ting - ing. Go

ev - er us be - fell. Then
now the corpse is bring - ing. Make

we may ring his knell. { Ding dong.
all the bells are ring - ing. {

GROUND

Ting, ting

113

W. Lawes (1652)

She weep - eth sore

tears are on her

_____ and her vir - - gins are

all her lov - ers she_____ hath_____

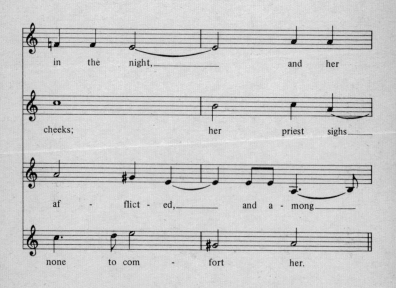

in the night,_____ and her

cheeks; her priest sighs_____

af - flict - ed,_____ and a - mong_____

none to com - fort her.

162

Anon. (1652)

1. The sil - ver swan, who liv - ing had no
2. wise.

throat. Lean - ing her breast a - gainst the reed - y

more: Fare-well all joys,___ O___ death come close mine

note, Till death ap - proached, un - locked her si - lent

shore, Thus sung___ her first and last___ and sung no

eyes. More geese than swans now live, more fools than

163

H. Lawes (1652)

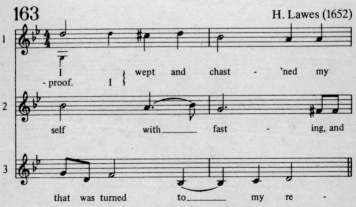

- proof. I { wept and chast - 'ned my

self with___ fast - ing, and

that was turned to___ my re -

164

1. O Ab - sa - lom, O Ab-sa- -lom, my son, my___ son, Ab - sa - lom.

2. O Ab - sa - lom, my son, my son, O Ab-sa-lom, my son, my son. Would

3. God I had died, would God I had died, would God I had died for thee.

165

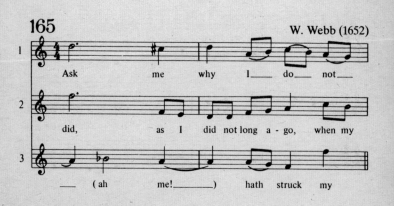

1. Ask me why I___ do___ not___

2. did, as I did not long a - go, when my

3. ___ (ah me!_____) hath struck my

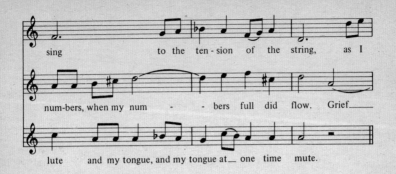

sing to the ten-sion of the string, as I

num-bers, when my num - - bers full did flow. Grief____

lute and my tongue, and my tongue at__ one time mute.

166

C. King (1763b)

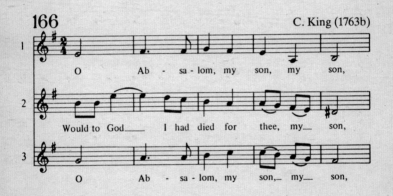

1. O Ab - sa - lom, my son, my son,

2. Would to God____ I had died for thee, my__ son,

3. O Ab - sa - lom, my son,__ my__ son,

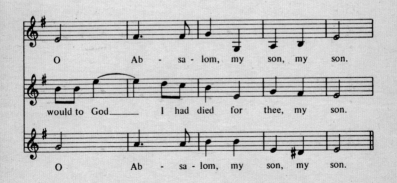

O Ab - sa - lom, my son, my son.

would to God____ I had died for thee, my son.

O Ab - sa - lom, my son, my son.

Appendix 1

THE ROUND FORM AND ITS HISTORY

1. Form and Development

A round is traditionally defined as a type of vocal canon. In all canonic music a second voice imitates the first, more or less closely, at the same or a related pitch and after a short interval in time. In a round, the imitation is exact and at the same pitch. In addition, and this is what distinguishes it from a canon in unison, the entry of each voice divides the music into sections of equal length. In England, two types of round developed within this general form, the continuous round and the sectional round. The method followed in singing rounds determined which of these two forms predominated.

The earlier method (still advocated in Hilton's *Catch that Catch Can*, 1652) was for each voice to sing the whole round right through a set number of times. A round sung in this manner opens with a section-long solo for the first voice and builds up slowly, section by section, to a longer passage for all the voices singing together. The number of voices then diminishes again equally slowly, section by section, leaving the last section also to be sung by one voice alone. With this method of singing, a round is most effective if the first and last sections sound like the opening and closing phrases of a melody. This criterion was often met by the unknown composers of the rounds in Ravenscroft's 1609 and 1611 collections, more rarely by Hilton and his fellow composers. A polyphonic style is particularly suited to this form of composition (for example, No.4), but the more general characteristic of the earlier period was simply that the music was continuous, reaching a close only at the end of the last section (as in Nos. 5, 6, 12, 43, 45 and 125). A common feature of the continuous round is that the internal phrasing does not coincide with the section boundaries. A particularly exciting example is 'She weepeth sore' (No. 161) by William Lawes; this consists of a continuous melodic line in which suspensions dramatically conceal the point where each new section begins. Some rounds make use of this flexibility to complete the harmonic cadence, not at the end of the sections, but by their opening notes (Nos. 4, 47 and 150). In yet another variant of the continuous round the last phrase leads straight on to the first, giving a circular melodic form (Nos. 7, 22 and 144).

The later method of singing rounds was to start in turn, as before, but to finish all together as soon as the first voice had sung the round through three times. This introduced a new pressure for phrase and cadence to match the section, for the method is only effective when all sections of the round contribute to a cadential close. The result was a discontinuous round in which a pause and an implied cadence marked the end of each section. With this method of singing, only the first section is ever heard alone. The temptation is then to construct a sectional round as if the first section represented a melody and the later ones its accompaniment. The rationale for resisting this is more social than musical: the round was, and remained, music for equal companions to sing; and that sense of equal value had still to be represented in each section. One can see this equalizing process at work in Purcell's 'I gave her cakes' (No. 24), a three-part sectional round of great charm and beauty. The first and second voices open with intertwining melodic phrases from which, when sung together, a tune appears that seems to alternate between them. This tune is then given to the third voice, which takes it triumphantly to the final cadence.

The association between the method of singing and the round type is only partly historical: sectional rounds do appear in Ravenscroft's collections (e.g. Nos. 46, 79, 81 and others) and form the majority in Hilton's. In Playford's first collection after the Restoration, however, there were only three new continuous rounds (of which two are Nos. 22 and 135), and by the end of the century (1701), none. Typically the continuous round was short; it might have three to ten voices, but its section lengths ranged only from one to five bars. The transition to the sectional form made possible the development of longer and more complex sections, such as those of Purcell. No further essentially different form of round developed. Some composers took advantage of the antiphonal possibilities latent in the round form, as in 'Hold thy peace' (No. 83) or the dialogues by Thomas Arne (for an example, see No. 139); and also as in the occasional cases of *double entendre* (Nos. 14, 33, 107 and 112). In all other respects, rounds reflect the basic musical style of their period and the ability (or otherwise) of their composers.

2. History

The earliest known round is, of course, 'Sumer is icumen in' (No. 119), from a thirteenth-century manuscript. When Charles Burney transcribed it (1776) he commented, 'The chief merit of this ancient composition is the airy and pastoral correspondence of the melody with the words. As to the modulation, it is so monotonous, that little more than two chords are used throughout the canon. But being the first example of counterpoint in six parts, as well as of canon, fugue or catch that can be produced, it seems to form an aera in vocal harmony and to merit the reader's attention.' Later authorities have questioned the exact date and the significance of the notation (Bukofzer; Schofield), but not the fact that it is a round, even if surprisingly early. To judge by later manuscript collections, it seems likely that rounds flourished alongside other canonic forms and in an oral tradition as well as at court (Stevens). Rounds are freely quoted and sung in Shakespeare's plays. In *Twelfth Night* the Clown, Sir Andrew Aguecheek and Sir Toby Belch give a drunken rendering of 'Hold thy peace' (No. 83), an example that demonstrates both its popularity and the informal nature of the occasions on which it might be sung.

The seventeenth century saw the heyday of the round. The first collection of rounds to be published was Ravenscroft's *Pammelia*, which appeared in 1609. No composers were given and some of the rounds can be found in earlier manuscript collections (e.g. Nos. 5, 6, 45 and 82). Ravenscroft explained in his preface that he published them 'that all might equally partake of that which is so generally affected', or, as we might put it today, to meet popular demand. Another major collection appeared during the Commonwealth (1652) and this time the editor, John Hilton, was one of the composers. After the Restoration Hilton's publisher, John Playford, produced a whole series of collections of catches, each one being extensively revised to include the latest compositions. At the beginning of the century most of the rounds were short and memorable. By the mid-century, however, we find that the rounds in Hilton's collection were not only longer but apparently intended to be read from the printed page rather than sung by ear. If the earliest composers were anonymous, later the most prolific composers of rounds were also the great composers of their day, like William Lawes and Henry Purcell. The round – or catch, as it was then called – had reached a Golden Age.

Incidentally, there is no suggestion at this time that a catch was different in form from a round; rather, the word 'catch' simply displaced the word 'round' as the general term for the form of music. To Ravenscroft the terms were interchangeable, and the word 'round' appeared in the subtitle of the main collections until the end of the seventeenth century. By then, rounds were very much light entertainment and the sad or philosophical round was a rare thing (see section VII). Religious topics appeared in separate collections; for example, Playford (1667) announced a separate volume to cover 'canons, Gloria Patris and other Divine Hymns for three and four voices'. When in the next century religious texts reappeared in Warren's collections, they were labelled 'sacred rounds', while a round on any other topic was labelled 'a catch'. The connotations of the word catch, then, derived from its secular subject matter rather than its form.

In the eighteenth century the round form became a musical backwater. For many years the younger Playford's collection of 1701 provided the nucleus of the repertoire (see Appendix 2: Walsh, 1731 and 1762). The next major source of new rounds was the Noblemen's and Gentlemen's Catch Club. This was founded in 1761 and its secretary, Thomas Warren, produced a series of some thirty collections of 'canons, catches and glees', almost all being composed by the members. In 1763, young James Boswell, a protégé of the Earl of Eglinton who was one of the founders of the Catch Club, wrote in his journal, 'My Lord [Eglinton] made me very welcome, and immediately he and I began singing catches, which is really a most enlivening thing. There is some lively sentiment well accompanied with suitable music, and when sung in parts a fine harmony is produced. I take a lesson from him whenever I can' (Pottle, p 256). Ominously, however, Warren's first dedicatory page referred to 'this entertaining species of music, now almost buried in oblivion'. The round had become an obscure and obsolete form, preserved only by catch clubs.

It was still not obscure enough for some. Writing in the 1790s, William Jackson characterized catches as pieces which 'when quartered, have ever three parts obscenity to one part music'. He went on to damn the catch in every way: for being vulgar and obscene, for being an outmoded and barbaric form of music and, finally, for being sung out of tune and noisily by drunken performers. The passage can be found in Rimbault (1860), who quotes Jackson at length and approvingly. Topics such as drinking and sex had fallen into disfavour, which meant that although a private men's club could sing catches, polite society could not. Rimbault's idea was to revive the round by providing bowdlerized versions suitable for Victorian society. In his version, for example, Purcell's 'Once, twice, thrice I Julia tried, the scornful puss as oft denied,' became 'One, two, three, our number is right, to sing our song tonight'. His book was the first attempt to survey the history of the round and contains a useful biographical dictionary of the composers. Since he altered the music as well as the words, however, it is not a good guide to the rounds themselves. All too often, the form in which earlier rounds have come down to us in this century is his, and an unfortunate result has been the impression that English rounds are childish in tone or sentiment. In fact, as I hope this new collection shows, English rounds are as diverse in subject and approach as are, say, English folk-songs, and deserve to be at least as widely sung.

References

BUKOFZER, M., *Sumer is icumen in, A Revision*, University of California Publications in Music, Volume 2, No. 2, 1944.

BURNEY, C., *A General History of Music*, Vol. I, 1776; reprinted N.Y., Dover, 1957.

POTTLE, F., *Boswell's London Journal*, London, Heinemann, 1950.

RIMBAULT, E.F., *The Rounds, Catches and Canons of England*, London 1860.

SCHOFIELD, B., 'The provenance and date of "Sumer is icumen in"', in *Music Review*, 1948, Vol. 9.

STEVENS, J., 'Rounds and canons from an early Tudor songbook', in *Music and Letters*, 1951, Vol. 32.

(See also Appendix 2, Sources.)

Appendix 2

SOURCES

Note: The italicized title or subtitle is the one to use when consulting the *Catalogue of Early Printed Music* (London, British Library) for library holdings.

1609a	RAVENSCROFT, T.	*Pammelia* Musicks Miscellanie or mixed variety of pleasant roundelayes and delightful catches, of 3, 4, 5, 6, 7, 8, 9, 10, parts in one.
1609b	RAVENSCROFT, T.	*Deuteromelia*
1611	RAVENSCROFT, T.	*Melismata*
1652	HILTON, J.	*Catch that Catch Can,* or a choice collection of catches, rounds & canons for 3 or 4 voyces.
1667	PLAYFORD, J.	Catch that Catch Can, or the *Musical Companion.* Containing catches and rounds for three and four voyces.
1685	PLAYFORD, J.	Catch that Catch Can: or the second part of the *Musical Companion;* being a collection of new catches, songs and glees, never printed before.
1686	PLAYFORD, J.	*Ibid.:* the second edition.
1701	PLAYFORD, H.	The second book of the Pleasant *Musical Companion:* Being a choice collection of catches for three and four voices . . . Compos'd by Dr John Blow, the late Mr Henry Purcell, and other eminent masters. The fourth edition, corrected and much enlarged.
1702	PLAYFORD, H.	Supplement of new catches to the second book of the Pleasant Musical Companion.

1731	WALSH, I.	The *Catch Club* or Merry Companions, being a choice collection of the most diverting catches for three and four voices. Compos'd by the late Mr Henry Purcell, Dr Blow etc. (Volumes I and II).
1762	WALSH, I.	The *Catch Club* or Merry Companions. A collection of favourite catches for three and four voices by H. Purcell, Dr Blow, and the most eminent authors (Volumes I and II).
1763a, 1763b to 1794	WARREN, T.	*A collection of catches, canons and glees* (a second [– thirty-second] collection).
1769a	ARNOLD, J.	The *Essex Harmony*. . . being an entire new collection of . . . songs and catches, canzonets, canons and glees, for two, three, four, five and nine voices . . . Volume II.
1786a	ARNOLD, J.	The *Essex Harmony*. . . The third edition, with additions, etc. Volume I.

Index of Composers

Index of First Lines